So long, and thank you for all the waterproof mascara.

Sibling Rivalry Press, LLC
PO Box 26147
Little Rock, AR 72221

info@siblingrivalrypress.com

www.siblingrivalrypress.com

ISBN: 978-1-943977-77-2

Library of Congress Control No. 2019953151

By special invitation, this title is housed in the Rare Book and Special Collections Vault of the Library of Congress.

First Sibling Rivalry Press Edition, March 2020

"*Batman* comes on Television" previously appeared in *Stonewall Fifty: 21 Poets Connected by Arkansas on Queer Life after the Stonewall Riots* (Queer Arts Arkansas / Sibling Rivalry Press, 2019).

So long, and thank you for all the waterproof mascara.

Lilith Mae McFarlin

SIBLING RIVALRY PRESS

DISTURB / ENRAPTURE

LITTLE ROCK, ARKANSAS

CONTENTS

11   I Don't Have a Problem

13   I Wanna Punch the World in the Dick

15   It's Our First Date, and

18   *Batman* comes on television,

20   Another Day

23   Dear Teenage Me,

25   Afterwards

27   The Party's Getting Started

30   Straight Girl

33   I Stay Pretty Busy

35   Fuck

36   Men

38   So Long, and Thank You for All the Waterproof Mascara

41   Sloppy Ho Tan Lines

43   Digging

44   Please, Love Me

46   Being Cat-Called for the First Time

47   Things Can't Get Better

51   Just Another Thursday

53   Love is a Daffodil or Some Shit.

55   Pink Lips

58   Football Binary

59   You make me feel like doing a swan dive

61   Nightmare on Gender Street

64   Lonely, Lonely

66   Over Before It Begins Again

68   Concrete Eden

70   It Starts Like a Country Song

73   Pride

76   Ode to a Mullet

77   Gay Bacon Lettuce and Tomato

79   If You Need Me

81   Don't It Feel Like December

I DON'T HAVE A PROBLEM

I don't have a problem with straight people,
as long as they're not flamboyant.

If your sideburns are long,
    If you think Jesus had blue eyes,
If you wear your carabiner clip on the right
      and you don't know that means you're a bottom,

then your lifestyle is offensive
and I don't want you around children.

Because some little boy might see your tobacco-chewin' ass
and think it's okay to scratch his crotch mid-conversation.
Think it's okay to burn five gallons of gas, revving his F-250 engine.
Think it's okay to conceive children in the Golden Corral bathroom.

Axe Body Spray is not cologne.
Donald Trump does not belong on a child's birthday cake.
Don't ask me if I'm a fag or a dyke,
because I am both.

Peel that mud flap girl sticker off your bumper.
Burn the rebel flag that flies in your front yard.
Exfoliate and moisturize that face.
It looks like a graveyard for dead skin
with acne scar tombstones.

What kind of cisgender, heterosexual thing
do you got going on
down there?
Do you like it?
How do you have sex?

What's it like to walk alone at night,
hear a male voice,
and still feel safe?

I WANNA PUNCH THE WORLD IN THE DICK

I wanna punch the world in the dick,
because it's better than writing another poem
about crying into a perfectly good glass of Evan Williams.

I wanna punch the world in the dick,
because I feel like living another sad bourbon poem,

  after she told me she didn't want to see anymore
    or about getting laid because I'm sad
    or about being sad about not getting laid.

I wanna punch the world in the dick,
because there's not a Marlboro Red between my lips.
Never mind, there is a cowboy killer between my lips,
because this poem isn't some lie I told my doctor.

I wanna punch the world in the dick,
while I tune my banjo with my toes,
and use my free hand
to smash the patriarchy with a giant, semi-realistic dildo.

I wanna punch the world in the dick,
because guys can parade shirtless down the street
with their sagging, hairy guts bouncing
against the waistline of their basketball shorts.

Meanwhile, I'm over here with a moderately flat stomach,
getting arrested for wearing the same outfit.

  People used to be okay with me walking around topless.
  I wonder what's different.

I wanna punch the world in the dick,
because the police officer just stole the cowboy killer

right from between my chapped lips,
and now he's smoking it.

I wanna punch the world in the dick,
because some old lady just yelled that I could have at least
shaved my armpits before prancing around
next to a daycare, half-nekkid.

I just bought a new mascara.
Why couldn't she have just told me my eyelashes are pretty?

As the pig shoves me in the back of his patrol car,
I yell that female body hair isn't a crime.
I think Porky just said something
about that not being why he's about to lock me up in the redneck hotel.

I tell him I couldn't understand what he said over the smell of bacon.
He tells me to remind him to breathalyzer me when we get there.

I wanna punch the world in the dick,
because all I wanna do is write another poem
about being sad over some girl.
But all that happened this time was that she said no
when I asked her if she wanted to get tacos with me,

but I still wanna punch the world in the dick
because I spent my whole lunch break writing this poem.
I'm not going to jail.
I'm still a free slut.

After work, I think I'll go out and drink some Evan Williams,
tear up a little, and write another poem about that.

IT'S OUR FIRST DATE, AND

I walk in and she's already at the bar,
gracefully sipping a beer that has an amber tone
that suggests it's more expensive than my usual Budweiser.
Her accent has more twang than my banjo,
but the shaved half of her head and cardigan suggest bohemian-
a way with women.

She skips past hello like an ad in a magazine and asks,
"Do you want to sit at the bar, or go find a table?"
I tell her, table. I get my cheap beer.
I chose table because I wanted to study
the beginnings of lines forming on her face
that accent her cheekbones like I hope mine will someday.
I want to take in her outfit and mannerisms, the way she sits,
because she's been at this a lot longer than me.

Before transitioning, while dating,
I had to make sure the pitch of my voice
stayed below that of a great dane bark,
had to keep my wrist stiff like the arched back
of a panther ready to pounce.
You know, how a man is supposed to act,
only to eventually drop the act and become
a unicorn with frozen yogurt swirling from its ass.

Now, I sit across from her, gesturing with my hands
as if I have a sparkler in each, writing "femme"
in smoke until my fingertips burn.

She laughs with head-shaking nostalgia
when she notices the matching silver bands
on my middle and ring fingers,
the way you'd look at a photo from college
and wonder why you let someone take your picture
after that many Four Lokos.

She talks about her degree in gender studies.
She talks about giving her cat-callers the finger and getting away with it.
She even shook one man's ladder until she saw fear sweat down his face.
She talks about giving birth.

I place an open hand beneath the table,
just below my navel,
knowing the only way anything will grow there

is if I start drinking Budweiser every night again.
She's eaten half that nutty bird sandwich,
and her lipstick hasn't even faded.

She isn't rushed or swayed when the waitress asks us
over and over
if we need anything else,
trying to push us out the door as if we couldn't pay our check,
so that a man and woman may take our place.

She asks me what my favorite color is and I tell her its chartreuse,
which turns out to be the same as hers,
and her eyes are spotlights shining on the fact that I'm finally
dating someone like me, dating as myself.
Like a monarch sprouting from her cocoon to land on another monarch,
freshly back from her flight to Mexico, or wherever they migrate.

We pay and leave, going dutch like wooden clogs.
A great perk of dating now is not having to pay for everything.
We stand outside and smoke after. Three puffs in,
I switch my cowboy killer around in my hand
so it rests in the circle of my thumb and forefinger,
which is the way she holds it.
I hope she doesn't notice.

When the butts are stomped flameless beneath
our steel toe boots, we go next door to look at beauty products.
I pick out a ten dollar eyeshadow, which is a splurge for me.

She looks at lotions that cost twice as much,
telling me which ones are just cute packaging,
and which ones make you glow like a Christmas tree
that fell into the fireplace.
I say that I just exfoliate every once in a while,
and hope my face doesn't fall off.

I look back on everything I've said throughout the night,
and I feel as though I am a child with glue and marker on her hands,
putting on a jean jacket and sunglasses,
doing her best imitation of a teenager to impress the babysitter.

We buy what wound up in our hands, and we leave.
She says it was nice to meet me and she'll stay in touch,
which is what people say when they don't want a second date.
I look like someone just spat tobacco juice on my white sneakers.
I stand there for a minute, letting it sink in
that my chest will never curve against hers.

BATMAN COMES ON TELEVISION,

and the bare couch cushion is only a reminder
that you aren't there to watch it with me.

I have no reason to learn to cook fried okra or deviled eggs
instead of my usual microwave burritos,
because you can't exist.

In case anyone wants to know, for me,
this is the hardest part of being transgender.

I can't tell you how I watched the same movie
when I was little like you. I can't buy you a *Batman* coloring book
in hopes that you'll let me color the cape on at least one page,
and promise to color it your favorite midnight blue.

It's the middle of the day, and I need to lay in bed
to make this okay. My pillow is almost soft enough to make me forget
        my non-existent womb,
until I hear kids play outside my window, laughing and yelling,
and I wish you were there to help them save Gotham.

You're not there for me
to be strong enough not to cry.

My last-night's-makeup eyes drip black,
and I'm sure they look bruised.
Like both your knees from falling by the jungle gym.

I wish it was you crying on my shoulder because of that
or because the Tooth Fairy isn't real or
because of the burnt half of Two-Face's, well, face.

Instead, I lay here, ironically locked in the fetal position,
which only reminds me that my body is gravel,
and gravel is no place for seeds.

Nothing can grow in me.
I feel buried by my own rocky surface.

From the sidewalk outside,
I hear the children's laughter,
and each giggle reminds me
that you'll never call me your mother,
let alone your sidekick, Robin.

I want to feel you kicking inside of me.
I want to find space in my tiny, one-bedroom apartment for your crib.
I want an excuse to hang a Batman poster on my nicotine yellow wall
that my landlady won't let me paint.

Unlike the parents we all grew up with,
I promise I wouldn't give you a real hot toddy
as soon as you were old enough to sit up on your own,
even if this is Arkansas.

When it's the two weeks of actual winter we get around here,
I want to remind you to put on your jacket before you go out and play,
and you know that thing would have a mask built into the hood,
complete with bat ears and a utility belt screen-printed around the waist.

But instead, I have my own floral-patterned comforter
wrapped around me, each blooming rose
a crimson reminder of the little Bat Boy
        or Bat Girl or Bat Gender Non-Binary-identifying child
who can never flourish inside me.

ANOTHER DAY

of substitute teaching is about to begin.
The Nike squeaks on the hallway tile are muffled
by my closed door,
which I open as the bell rings-
a lie followed by my name written on the board,
"*Mr.* McFarlin."

They trudge in and sit down,
but won't stop screaming at each other.
I try to call roll:

Jasmine Adams,

                Here.

They throw paper balls and crayons at each other,
I yell for them to stop
to no effect
like they are a downhill bike with no brakes.

Err… Jackson Cummings,

                    here.

More paper balls fly
like high school grenades.
I pretend not to notice
as I shout their names.

Britoni Smith,

                here.

I finish, and pass out the assignment,
tell them to let me know
if there are any questions.

Ten hands pop up quicker than switchblades.

I call on the first one,
who asks what the other nine want to know:
"Are you a man, or a lady?"

I want to say that I am sometimes
a glittering bubble gum pink unicorn,
sometimes a shimmering teal octopus.

But, they probably haven't been taught about metaphors yet.
So I point to the name I stole from my drag king alter ego,
Mr. McFarlin.

They ask why I have long hair and purple nails.
I say, Because I like them that way.

They ask if it's because I am a rock star.
I say, If I was a rock star, I wouldn't be here.

They say most men paint their nails black.
I say, Yes they do,
focus on your assignment.

They ask if I'm gay.
I tell them they can ask the principal,
if they really want to know.

From behind my back,
"fag" jerks out of a fat boy's mouth.
I turn around and ask him what he said.

He shrugs,
while making a face that suggests
he's never spoken–
if only that were the case.

DEAR TEENAGE ME,

It is fucking amazing that your mohawk is so big
that you about have to stick your head
out your car window when you drive.
That spiky glory is held up with Elmer's glue,
so I bet the I-30 wind wouldn't even make it split or bend.
That is why I insist that you are my best self.

I love that you don't know why you insist
on sitting on your girlfriend's lap
instead of the other way around.
I love that you try to hold a boy's hand
every time he calls you a fag.

I love that you give yourself the same Sharpie tattoos every day.
I still do that, even though I'm well on my way
to being smothered and covered in real ones
like hash browns with daddy issues.

I still have your Alien Sex Fiend T-Shirt and
I might be wearing it right now.
It goes great with the grim reaper tattooed on my arm.

I still call the president Fascist.
Believe it or not, they will elect
a giant Cheeto with a bad weave,
and that Cheeto will make Dick Cheney
look like Kathleen Hanna.

I love that all of your clothes are ripped apart
and safety-pinned back together.
I love that you stuck up for Curtis when
those camouflage-fetish,
Skoal in the underage lip
        white boys
told him he wasn't black enough.

I love that you don't care that you're a terrible guitar player.
I'm sorry that you grow up to fish,
drink Evan Williams, and play the banjo.

I'm sorry that you have panic attacks
when you try to have sex and you don't know why.

I'm sorry that you lay in bed, crying, and wishing you were a girl,
and the world is still too cruel
to let you know that nothing is wrong with you.

I'm sorry that I accidentally slung
Manic Panic hair dye all over your Leftöver Crack T-Shirt,
which is how I'm sure most Leftöver Crack T-shirts are ruined.

But don't worry, I still plan on dismantling the Capitalist agenda.
It's on my list after the cis-hetero patriarchy and Michelob Ultra.

I love you. You're beautiful, and I'm not just saying that
because you're me.
Just remember, you are always enough.

Yours truly and futurely,

You from the Future.

P.S. You're skinnier than me, so fuck you.

AFTERWARDS

We're laying in my bed,
her head on my shoulder.
My arm cradles her back.
She asks me what my last relationship was like.

I ask her if she means romantic.

Our pillow talk has become the cushion
for a pair of crash test dummies in a Subaru.
The silence feels worse than my breath smells.

I've forgotten about how sore my jaw is.

We got dinner first,
which is what I do when I don't want
to feel like a slut.

I guess I've led her on, since I took the time
to find out she loves both Bikini Kill and Brad Paisley as much as I do-
that she's a Virgo and a fake blonde.

I tell her that I'm tired and I need to rest up for tomorrow.
She gets up. I fucking hate
that she knows what that means.

I tell her I'm sorry, I'm just emotionally unavailable.
She says nothing as she puts on
the stripped-down, acoustic version of her previous outfit.
I'm emotionally unavailable, but part of me
wants to mend her every scar with the tip of my tongue.

As she trudges out the door, I apologize again.
Her last words to me are,
"You tops are all the same."

I stay up for two hours after she leaves,
pacing with a low-ball glass in my hand,
wondering how I could do that to another woman.

THE PARTY'S GETTING STARTED

No one has to know we've been on a few dates.
She's never told me that I'm beautiful,
but I still want her lipstick mouthed across my collarbone.

Someone's fingertips click the bass
into thudding through stereo speakers.
We've all gulped hellfire shots of Heaven Hill vodka over our tongues.
We disco like horny morons.

I grind on her until some guy switches off the lights.
I turn around and shake my ass,
and she's on it like she's a Buick tailgating my Honda in traffic.
I've had a rough day,
and I want her to thrust into me,
just so I'll have a reason to scream.

I stare through the door across the living room, towards a half-made bed.
I have visions of her fingers spiraling through my hair,
with my head between her thighs.

The song fades out and she fades away with it.
She's the redneck vodka in my body.

I step up to the counter,
and pour more booze in my Solo cup.
I add tonic water and a lime,
which is enough to mask the five-dollar taste.

Someone lost their cellphone and they turn the lights on to look for it.
I put ice in my drink, and I turn to face the party.

Now that it's bright enough for everyone to see again,
she's hanging all over her ex-boyfriend
like barbecue sauce on pulled pork,

even though he ignores her, laughing with some guy in a mesh tank top.

I tell myself that she's just drunk, and I can forget this,
until she kisses him on the cheek.
His conversation isn't even interrupted,
and he doesn't seem to care. But I do.

I dirty dance on everyone in the room,
making fake love to everyone,
including her ex-boyfriend-
and I top him,
like fire on a mountain of tires.
She clings to him again, but keeps her eyes on me.

I ask myself why I thought she would want
to be with a trans girl when she could be with a guy.
At least I emasculated this one.
Still, he has it so good.
No wonder I used to tell myself I wasn't a girl.

Another girl puts her arm around me.
She says, "Let's go snuggle," and she pulls me
into the same bedroom that I planned on visiting earlier.

We lay there, my head on her shoulder,
my breasts pushed into her side.
We're in full view of everyone.

A few people have even wandered in to talk,
when my bullshit dancing partner pries herself off her ex-boyfriend
long enough to come glare at us. I look up at her.

I haven't even been kissed yet, and I'm not sure I want to,
but no one has to know that.
I ask if she needs to talk to me.
She says, "That's not wrong or inappropriate or anything."
I say, "I'm not your fucking girlfriend."

She stomps away as her fists clench tighter than my skinny jeans.
I get up in time for her to hug everyone except me as she leaves,
walking along the pot smoke pathway
created by the headlights through the open door.

I think about following her,
then I laugh at the idiot I am as the door slams.

After she's gone, my guy friend takes me outside,
onto the cold sidewalk.
He tells me he's sensed what's going on,
being careful in bringing up the specific.

He tells me she left because she's confused.
I tell him that I couldn't care less, and I wish that was the truth.
I spend a worrisome amount of time
in the bathroom as the bass thuds on.

I can't help but find her picture on my phone.
I'm sitting there with my pants around my ankles,
staring at her sharp, arresting jawline and her olive eyes.
I think of how she can make me laugh,
even when I've just burst into tears
over my dead best friend.

How I wish I was hers.

STRAIGHT GIRL

How come you were only queer
when it was just you and me?
How come
when we went from coffee dates to getting dinner,
all you wanted to talk about was hanging with your ex-boyfriend?

I was the one who held your hair
while you puked
because you drank too many
of those pineapple upside-down shooters
after he dumped you.

I know that entitles me to nothing.
It's just for perspective.

He's always talking about how big his dick is,
and I don't care,
because I can fucking buy a bigger one.

You hugged me that night after dinner,
tried to put your head on my chest,
but then I let go.

I tried asking you out again anyway,
and you were just too busy for me.
Not for everyone else.

I fucked someone else's brains out,
but you were in my head the whole time.

When we went to the same parties,
after two vodka sodas, you'd tell everyone
how you weren't into girls,
but if you were,

you'd be into _____, _____, _____,
         & _____.

After four, I overheard you say how much my
muscle shirt and blue eyeliner made you want to fuck me.

Honey, you're like a swimming pool.
If I drink enough gin and smoke a little corn,
I might jump in.

But I could never be wasted enough
to swallow your water on my way to the bottom.

When I was a child, I told the swimming lessons lady I was a girl,
and she laughed and told me I was wrong.
Her eyes were chlorine blue like yours,

and chasing you has made me feel wrong for being a girl-
wrong for wanting another girl.
Maybe if you'd met me a few years back,
you could have fallen in love the boy I pretended to be,
even with my drag king goatee.

I could have tasted your dusty rose lipstick.

You could've even kept those damn fingernails.

Maybe you're not into girls.
Maybe you're not into boys.
Maybe "sexually fluid" is code for
a straight girl who went to liberal arts college.

I'm maybe a shitty person for saying that.
There's different levels of outness.
There's different levels of outness and your elevator is stuck
on the first one.

I may have been wrong for chasing you,
when love should come easy instead of not at all.
I want someone who thinks it's sexy when I read my poetry,
who takes me fishing.

I'm not perfect.
I say cunt way too much,
and give cops the finger when they're not looking.

But I will never be anyone's experiment.
I will never be anyone's phase.

It's better for me to sit here without you,
where I'll be sad and cunty for a while
in my penthouse level of unapologetic queerness.

I'll fight the urge to leave my apartment
and buy a bottle of rot-gut,
and I'll watch romantic comedies and
cry during the obligatory *walking in the rain* scenes.

I'll do this until I fall asleep on the gap in my bed
where I used to wish you were.

Then I'll wake up to the roses I never gave you,
hanging by their toes from my ceiling fan.
They're starting to get dusty,
but they look like another woman's lips.

I STAY PRETTY BUSY

My love for her is a plastic spork
that I stabbed through my stomach,
and left there this morning.

Even though it hurts,
it's fun to bounce Fritos off of it
into a bowl of chili and cheese, and
pretend like they're kids on a diving board.

I splash back to the reality of a lunch gone cold,
followed by the end of my break.
I clock back in, and we work the front desk together.

She shows me some graphic design-y thing she made on the computer,
and I want to hold her from behind.

Even if it was workplace-appropriate,
I know my snuggles would be rejected.
Still, the spork pierces deeper into my stomach
like it's pressed against her back.

I feel creepy for wanting her,
as if it were cringier
than watching this blood and Frito chili pie
splat down from my stomach.
I wonder why no one screams,

calls an ambulance,
or pukes up whatever cheeseburger
they ate so we can compare secretions.

She looks not at my gushing abdomen,
but at my grimace and she makes funny faces at me until I laugh.
This not only works when I'm about to cry,
but when I have a utensil penetrating my internal organs.

Someone walks by the desk
and says they like my eyeliner.
I say, "What about my gaping wound that shits comfort food?"

I look over to my co-worker.
The pain in my stomach rises like exploding
cheese bubbles in the microwave.
She renews what she said weeks ago
when I asked her if she wanted to get tacos sometime:

"We'll have to figure out when. I stay pretty busy.
We'll have to figure out when. I stay pretty busy.
We'll have to figure out when. I stay pretty busy.
We'll have to figure out when. I stay pretty busy."

The first time, it felt like the "W" at the end of "Arkansaw"
turned into an "S," and my kneecaps dissolved.

This was her response, even though we'd been drunk together.
This was her response, even though I thought we were friends.

She's not a shitty person for not wanting to date me.
I'm not entitled to the seat across from hers.
But I thought I deserved the words, "I like being your friend, but…".

Instead, she made me feel like a stranger
who leaked blood and cheese on her pink sweater,
and I felt just as bad. And I still feel just as bad.
I will always be sorry that I love her.

Tomorrow, I'll shove the spork back under my ribs,
spread a thin, gooey smile over the pain,
and head off to work.

FUCK

If fuck were a person, Fuck would raise her fist
and shout, "Smash the patriarchy" and, yes, her
unshaven armpit hair would be dyed neon
pink. Fuck would play guitar in a punk band called,
"Every Woman Adores a Fascist"; she'd moonlight
in a Feminist rap group and, yes, "the 'hood"
is short for "Planned Parenthood." She'd smell like dank weed;
sing like a tiger's roar through a megaphone.

If I got to know Fuck,
I'd say, "I love you."
She'd say, "Love is a Patriarchal conspiracy. Even if it's between women."
I'd sing, "Rebel girl, you are the queen of my world."
She'd say, "That's a little better."

MEN

I can't stop thinking about the creepy man
I helped at my job. He made me feel the pendant
on the end of his necklace,
telling me it wasn't cheap, telling me to take note of how
          hard
it was- *it* being the TV-friendly version of his dick.

I wouldn't know what to do with the real one
if it was in my face.

He tells me we need to have a drink sometime,
and that I should go to the Super 6 Motel tonight
and ask for him.
He doesn't have a cell phone right now.
I want to tell him,
"Sorry, I only fuck at the Double Tree."

But I'm at my job, so I thank him
and tell him to have a nice day.

I can't tell if he's a tranny chaser, or a straight man.
I'm not sure which one is more likely
to stab me and leave me in a bathtub
if I said yes.

He didn't tell me it's sexy
that I don't shave my arms,
so I'm thinking straight guy.

Next, I help a man
who told me that he believes that Elvis is alive
and Paul McCartney got flattened
by a Buick way back in the sixties.
Some actor has been posing as Paul
since John and Ringo dropped acid and fingered a sitar.

He doesn't tell me any of this, actually,
he tells it to my tits,
even though I'm wearing a sports bra.

He tells my chest he thinks it's crazy
that these guys pulled such a fast one on him,
that he had a poster of a fake Beatle on his wall growing up.
I feel thumbtacked to the ceiling above his bed.

Men get away with that,
yet every accidental boob-glance I make,
I feel like the predatory tranny
all the Republicans are trying to keep out of public restrooms.

SO LONG, AND THANK YOU FOR ALL
THE WATERPROOF MASCARA

I'm crying so hard, I have to hold my face over the trash.
You know I hate to make a mess-
even though this waste basket has been overflowing since Christmas,
and now it's so hot, I've forgotten what sweaters look like.

Lord, am I getting that empty Lean Cuisine box all soggy.
I ate that microwave dumpster pasta the other day,
after I cried in the fetal position,
      in an empty bath tub,
          wearing low-rise, leopard print stretch pants
          and a seashell bra.

After a while, I wasn't crying because no one loves me.
I cried because I was sobbing, moderately fully-clothed
in a fucking bathtub.

That's in my top ten most pathetic cry moments,

along with that time Stacy invited me over to her duplex
to *watch a movie*. We all know what that means.

She picked The Lion King, which was kind of weird.
When Mufasa died and Simba's all, "Dad, wake up,"
tears ran marathons down my face like I was lying
moderately fully-clothed in an empty bathtub.
No one got finger-banged that afternoon.

Mufasa and Darth Vader were voiced by the same guy-
James Earl Jones- which ruins both movies for me,
if I think about it.

Sometimes, I relate way too much to Luke
in the "No, I am your father" scene.
I'm holding on to the edge of life's metal walkway, crying.
Instead of a cyborg in a black cape, it's the fact that I can't find a job,

so I can't move out of my transphobic parents' house
or afford a pair of floral Doc Martens.
I'm forced to live in a place where I'm misgendered
while REO Speedwagon wails in the background,
sounding like a Pixar movie where a bottle of Quaaludes comes to life
and learns to play guitar.

I can't find a job because, like a twenty-six-year-old
golden retriever puppy,
I have no experience.
Where do you get three years of experience for an entry level job?
Soon, I might have to dust off my red stilettos and start hookin'.
I'll give sobbing, puking handjobs all over town.
I'll stand on the street corner like a bicycle in a toy store window
and, when a john pulls up in his Nineteen Ninety-Three Toyota Corolla,
I'll walk up to that scumbag's window and say,
"Hey, baby. Want me to cry on that dick?"

If his dick's not gross enough to be cry-worthy,
I'll just think about the fact that I haven't had a girlfriend since
I was young enough to actually enjoy Corona,
the Barbie Jeep of beers.

But his dick will be gross enough,
because dicks are so much skin in one place—
like a radioactive skin tag.
We should all just have pussies, like birds.

If I was a Blue Jay, I'd do a fly-cry.
My tears would evaporate on the way down from the sky,
so no one would know I lived a sad life,
then I'd probably fly into a plane engine or some shit.

SLOPPY HO TAN LINES

I would say that I'm more butch than most straight men,
and more femme than most straight women.
I am the crimson lipstick stain
around the mouth of that Jim Beam bottle-
in this bar that's so divey, a box cutter
just magically appeared in my sock.

I would say that my body's in an in-between phase.
The girl parts are the catfish frying in the kitchen,
while the boy parts are a to-go box of pulled pork,
forgotten in the backseat of a Camaro.

I would say that there's too much of this and that to date
the strictly gay or straight, so I learned to spot bisexual women
from all the way across the room.
Example: a lady who has long fingernails,
but also calls her fists Tegan and Sara.

But I'm shy, so I wear a wallet chain and my sluttiest tank top
when I go out and hope for the best,
hoping they'll see my I-can't-believe-she's-not-cis-hips,
and ignore my sloppy ho' tan lines.
Like a skeeter-filled screen door at Meemaw's house,
the tank top is practically see-through.
Hopefully someone will want to pre-order my pussy.

I'll have to wait for them to talk to me first.
What would be my opening line, anyway?
"Hey, baby, are you into adults who still wear an A cup?"

A couple of bourbon Diet Cokes into the evening
would be the best time for them to approach.
I'll be sure to mention that I live by myself and get oh-so-lonely,
glossing over the fact that my genitals make me cry and throw up-

the fact that I am required to think of a cold black taser
as the perfect accessory to the swirling lilac dress I don't wear.

When we get back to my apartment with its beautiful popcorn ceiling,
the real show is about to start. We walk past my closet
full of dresses I don't wear because I'm single,
and we get nekkid almost right away.
Not naked, because that's what happens at the doctor's office.

Unlike the doctor's office, she'll let me leave my tucker
and my pink unisex briefs on,
because she's been with girls like me before.
Because what's underneath would turn my breathing
into the bull beneath a rodeo clown if I tried to use it sexually.

Even if it weren't for that, I've been on hormones for months,
so I have to strap one on that looks more like an anorexic bowling pin.
But first it's a lot of mouths and hands. She looks away from me briefly,
towards my first-place plaque that reads, *Fingerbang Championship 2010*.

After my pillow is layered with her moans and tears like a sex parfait,
she'll ask me if I want her to return the favor
like it's a leaf blower borrowed from a neighbor.

I take a couple of hits from the jar
of cranberry moonshine on my nightstand,
hesitate to release it from my fingertips, and say, Sure.

With the lights off and the covers disguising
the disgusting Elephant Man deformity between my Estradiol thighs,
I can do this. With her on top of me,
I feel safe, if even just for a little while.

DIGGING

I reach across my twin-size mattress for her, but my arm just falls against my comforter. I pull it back, and I can't see her. I dip my head over the edge of my mattress and look underneath my bed, but all I see is my sneaker collection. I throw each pair aside, and all that's behind them is carpet and the fucking wall. But I know she must be in my bed. Her breasts must press against mine. My lips must suck along her long, delicate neck. I can't lay without her bare embrace. I flip my body around, my head facing the foot of the bed, my legs spread over the headboard. I am a woman with needs. I crawl on my stomach, as if I am in boot camp and barbed wire could scrape the chemically blonde mullet from my skull if I don't squirm low enough across the sheet, underneath my comforter. If I can just find her hand, I can pull her back to the surface, roll her underneath me. Dip back under just enough to run the tip of my tongue around her clitoris, place my fingers in her wet cunt. I'll give her my whole fist, if that's what she wants and I'll never even ask for it back. I crawl and I crawl, and the tips of my toes feel as though they've not met the air for miles. My fingertips feel the end of my mattress, and it's cold, not wet, warm, and rough. My fingertips reach the end of my mattress, and I know what must be done. With my teeth and my hands and my tongue, I penetrate the fabic wall of my bed. I pull the hole wide enough to fit my head, and then my shoulders. I dig through springs piercing red, seeping cracks along the soft of my inner wrists. I keep going until I am to weak and dizzy to stay awake. Reluctantly, I sleep. I sleep without her, same as every fucking night.

PLEASE, LOVE ME

I sulk past the flower shop, and I can't help
but think of the irony that flowers symbolize new life,
but these are dead, decapitated from their nourishing roots.

Petals litter the floor inside, peak from underneath the glass door.
I see the Mother's Day flower arrangements
and wish I was the woman buying one.
My mother says she doesn't know me,
even though she held my hands when I was learning how to walk.

I see the white lilies, and wish I had a woman to buy them for,
a woman I could take home to meet my mother
who says she doesn't know me.
She is uncomfortable with me dating women,
but she thinks I'm a guy, so I feel like that should be okay.

I keep walking, even though my shoes
feel like they're sinking into the concrete sidewalk.
I see a mother and daughter laughing,
stepping through the entrance of a Mexican restaurant.
        The logo painted on the window is a sombrero,
            held up by some Spanish word that I think means spicy.

I want to know what that feels like,
having female kinship with one's mother.
Instead, I feel like I'm the only one who showed up to a fiesta.
At least I get to have all the Coronas to myself.

I want to be a liar, a manipulator,
        a
        straight
        man,
and everything she thinks I am, just so I can beg

her forgiveness and we can be close again.
I would admit to driving my car into a hotdog stand,
sending bratwurst flying down the choking throats
of ten dying innocent bystanders
just to get her to look me in the eye.

I want to plead with her,
Please, love me.
Please,   love me.
Please,   love   me.

But we've been through too much,
like a Walmart sack that got over-stuffed
with cans of chili
and busted right there in the damn parkin' lot.
The chili was half-off because the cans were dented
before they hit the ground,
and now a good deal is a brown stain next to a Ford Focus.

I try to get chili metaphors off my mind
as I unclip my keys from the left side of my waist,
and I unlock my car.

I am not wrong, I am a woman.
I am not a shitty person for being queer.
They dyed Goldfish crackers
rainbow for people like me.

As I open the door and turn to sit in the driver's side,
I feel something in my shoe.
I pull out a tulip petal,
and I stare at it in the palm of my hand,
and I know this isn't over.

BEING CAT-CALLED FOR THE FIRST TIME

My cousin had just dyed my hair so pink
that unicorns begged me for beauty tips.
I had just discovered eyebrow pencil
like a creek in the middle of the desert.

My mascara made my eyelashes so long
that they touched my windshield.
I was stuck at a stoplight that took longer
than the line at the DMV,
when a Ford Mustang pulled up next to me.

If you drive a Ford Mustang,
you're saying to the world,
"I'm not broke enough to justify it,
but the only shirts I own
are a Kroger six pack of wife beaters.
Yes, I call them 'wife beaters.'"

I heard laughter that was saltier
than the sweat drizzling down
the backs of the morbidly obese
as they ride their scooters into Walmart.

The driver of the Mustang rolled down his window
and said, "Hey, Baby."
He made clownfish kissy faces at me
as he flashed a backseat-wrinkled scrap of a napkin
with his phone number scribbled across it.

I kept my hands on the wheel,
and turned my eyes back towards the changing light.

THINGS CAN'T GET BETTER

My eyes open, and I'm already crying
like Bukowski without a bar stool.

Out of the puddle of drool on my pillow
splooshes a rainbow octopus tentacle.
I try to get up, but the tentacle reaches out
and twists around my hair, squeezing it into a ponytail.

Then it jerks my head back down onto the pillow.
I belong here like old bobby pins
and moldy Cheetos belong underneath a couch.
I'm stuck here against my will,
but my legs don't flail, like the legs of a roadkill party clown.

I'm too sad to care about the tentacle holding my head to my pillow,
which has eased up a bit.
At least I can't get up and drink
that antifreeze milkshake sitting on my dresser.

Just kidding, it's on my bedside table,
and I'm spooning it down my throat.
Don't worry, there's vodka in there, too.

I put the spoon in my mouth again,
but now it's warm and empty like it's been sitting out for hours.

I look down past the edge of my mattress
like a kid checking for a monster's tail poking out from underneath,
and the milkshake glass lays, shattered in front of my nightstand.

I look at the spoon in my hand, then at the matching one on the floor,
buried in broken glass like a rose in the snow.
My hair falls back into my face as the rainbow tentacle lets go
and waves goodbye like I'm aboard a cruise ship.

But there's no streamers and confetti when you kill yourself.

I stand up and wonder why I'm still holding onto the spoon.
I throw it down, and as soon as I hear it pat against the carpet,
I feel the public school cafeteria-grade metal
between my thumb and forefinger.

I stammer past my plastic Christmas tree,
which I've left up for fifteen years and counting,
like my bedroom has yuletide priapism.

The door is only open enough for a small dog to fit through,
and I try to pull it all the way open,
but the hinges might as well be welded together.

I squeeze through the opening as the doorknob
attempts to penetrate my navel.
I blink and I'm at the top of the stairs.
The empty canister of antifreeze lay at the foot,
leaving a trail of rainbow puddles on the steps.

I follow them like a spider propelling
down the ropey gunk shooting out its ass.
And I'm at my own funeral.

My family didn't spring for a casket, so my body
is just propped up in the corner
like your uncle after too much Wild Turkey.
My binded chest is covered by a suit,
and my long hair is shaved into a crew cut.

The front row is my parents and siblings
in folding chairs with chipped, tan paint.
They're all wearing buttons with a pre-transition photo of me on them.

They hang on to that drag king goatee,
thick from hair dye rather than purely follicle,
like it's a clean syringe in a dirty back alley.

Behind them are all my matches
from OkCupid-dot-com,
 and every one of them is lit.

Their part of the room is an inferno
of tequila shots and Camel Crush smoke.
BiCurious_SoccerMom85 needs to be rolled on her side,
so she doesn't choke on her own vomit.

I ignore my desecrated corpse,
which isn't hard, despite the unembalmed smell.

I join the party, trying to excuse myself past KinkyKat93 and
TacoBitch420
          and they don't move
          and they don't even turn their heads to look at me
          and I'm even more invisible than usual
          and my grimace turns into a confused frown.

I squeeze my way towards the middle through spaces
between backs and breasts.

In the center of the party,
the eye of the storm, surrounded by a wall
of mostly chubby twenty-somethings
is a stool with a shot of vodka on the seat.

I place my finger tips around it, and lift it towards my lips,
only to hit myself around the mouth with my empty hand.

The vodka sits where it was before as my teeth ring like a tuning fork.
I can't stand the sound as my eyes close
and my hand slaps over my mouth,
trying to hold my teeth still to stop the ringing.

When my eyes open again,
a woman in an Easter Bunny costume stands before me.
There's a joint in her mouth,

well, the one on the mask, anyway.
She says, "No one will ever love you,
and your family won't accept you
if you kill yourself.
Things can't get better if they don't continue."

JUST ANOTHER THURSDAY

I got hit by a big rig. It didn't hurt
that bad. The damn thing didn't stop. It bolted
down the road with me, well, splayed across the grill.

My swoopy, platinum blonde hair turned into water bugs that
crawled down and scraped the makeup off my face with their legs.
I felt them squirm back up to my scalp, parting into
brown, neatly-bombed and short masculinity.

I looked down, and my breasts flattened like DVD's
my dyke flannel. The earring fell out of my cartilage.

The exhaust jumped out of the
pipes on either side of the big rig, and came
together in the shape of a can of Skoal.

The Skoal smoke smelled like a cigarette threw up.
It floated into the legs of my skinny
jeans and stretched them into boot-cut Wranglers.

The smoke had a texture like rotten marinara
sauce. The smoke went down into my Chuck Taylors
and melted them into boots straight out of a

Spaghetti Western. The water bugs came back
down from the top of my head, and put a pair
of Convenience Store Aviators with a

cracked lens on my face. The crack was in the shape
of the Arkansas River. The big rig stopped
so fast, I flew off the front and landed face

down. I stood, and I managed to brush some of
the dirt off my clothes, then I looked up. I was
in front of Possum Joe's. I thought, What the hell?

I limped inside, and sat on a barstool. On
the counter, finger-written in the dust was,
Wash me. The bartender trudged up to the counter and

said, "What'll it be?" I said, "I'll have a vodka martini."
He growled, "That's a funny way of sayin', Bud Lite."

He kneeled down, he opened the refrigerator,
and I heard the sound of babies crying in
a tritone harmony. He sat a newborn on the counter,
and congratulated me on becoming a father.

He waits a moment and asks me why I haven't
touched my drink and I say,
"Because I didn't give birth to it.
I have to be the mother.
I have to be a mother."

He grabs the baby by the neck,
and throws it against the wall.
It shatters into a broken beer bottle.
I pick up a shard and run it from my palm
to my elbow. But I can't seem to bleed.

LOVE IS A DAFFODIL OR SOME SHIT.

Loneliness always makes love grow too quickly,
and crooked, so that the root weakly remains on my side of the garden,
where she can pull it out like a weed,
leaving its veins in my dirt.

I stay planted in front of my TV,
which waters my eyes and fertilizes my brain,
but my heart never grows past my own ribs.
My relationship status is:
"Takes up both cushions on her loveseat."

My loveseat, where I think of Frankie.
We were going to play guitars together
and we both have white Stratocasters,
so I thought it was meant to be.

I lit her cigarette without using my hands to shield the flame
from the cold, unseasonable April wind,
which killed the March flowers.
But the tobacco leaves in her cowboy killer were already dead.
The leaves were already dead,
then sprayed with addiction chemicals that made me want more.

But she quit me as soon
as the cowboy killer crushed flameless beneath her sneaker.
Like a Marlboro ad, I tried to get her attention the next day,
but she had quit me after the last night's puff,
without even needing the patch.

All it took was one smoke outside of a coffee shop,
where we read our poems.
Hers were worse than Satan's macchiato, anyway.

All it took for Sara was the new Star Wars,
and some tea at her place after.
We were Storm Trooper lasers that always miss.
The also dead leaves
at the bottom of my cup formed a question mark,
hers formed a slamming door,
like the one I disappeared behind—
never to buzz back through,
like a mosquito escaping the heat in June.

For Brenna, all it took was sushi,
octopus legs like fresh rubber bands in my mouth,
which she never held to hers.

Will my love life always be one-and-done, nothing but a bunch of
one-night-can't-stand to see me more than once?
Can you call it a love life,
if the daffodil gets ripped from the ground
before the neighbors even see it?

PINK LIPS

The walls are menstrual blood red,
and they're dripping and shedding themselves onto the white tile.
The party is packed like a new box of toothpicks
with cis women in puffy-skirted dresses
to the point that it looks like they're waist deep in a giant bubble bath.
My dress is tighter than lids on Tupperware
to the point of having to make sure I've tucked properly
every time I think no one is looking.

Everyone's champagne glass is refilled so regularly
that I haven't bothered looking at my watch since I got here.
I look through the window to my left,
and I see myself sitting in my living room,
with a blanket over my lap and my tits out,
watching Netflix and eating chicken wings.
There's buffalo sauce on my nipple, and I don't even care.

Meanwhile, Party Me keeps chatting it up
with some woman who smiles with every stale
egg yolk tooth in her mouth, leaking *young man*

between them like liquid from the bottom of a cheap trash bag.
I look down at my own champagne flute,
and estrogen pills cluster at the bottom,
reminding me I don't have ovaries.
In my reflection in its glass,

I see stag antlers growing from my forehead,
bookmarking my birth-assigned sex in this thick book of a crowd.

I feel above my head and one scrapes through the skin on my palm
like peeling a potato. I look at my hand,
and the color of my blood clashes
with the menstrual red walls like a child,
indiscriminately mashing its fists against piano keys.

The man comes by, refilling our champagne
from the mouth of a blonde, naked baby,
its bubbles fizzing in a tritone harmony
until they roar into the sound of infants crying.
I feel the muscles over my non-existent uterus tighten
like a gag during leather-whipped fucking,
muffling my useless safe word.

I imagine the child I should be able to birth,
my fingers running through her auburn hair.

I imagine staining her white, lacy bow
with the blood from my fingers.
The menstrual blood red walls slant inward,
looming over me like a pulpit
as I take my tranny communion.
The champagne washes estrogen pills down my throat.
They're chalky and sweet on my tongue.

My voice slips low into its original octave as I talk to
garbage juice lady in front of me,
sounding like a garbage truck with a broken axle.
My feet grow into hooves and break the stilettos I was wearing.

I try to focus on the tacky, cakey makeup
on the lady's face to keep from crying,
not on what she's saying.
Not my girthy hairy body,
her purple eyeshadow, and pink lips.

Purple eyeshadow, pink lips. I am the stag.
Purple eyeshadow, pink lips.
Purple eyeshadow, pink lips.
There's fur growing through my chest.

Purple eyeshadow.
The bulge between my thighs cannot be hidden.
Purple eyeshadow, pink lips.

Purple eyeshadow, pink lips.
Purple eyeshadow, pink lips.
I will always be a fake woman,
and not even bottom surgery can fix that.
Purple eyeshadow, pink lips.
Purple Eyeshadow, pink lips
pink lips pink lips pink

lips pink lips pink lips beef curtains pink lips pink
lips pink lips pink lips male genitals pink lips.
I am a lie.

FOOTBALL BINARY

Masculine is the mask you're in.
It's your helmet when
you pass pig skin and tackle men
to prove the weight of your dick
like bratwurst on a butcher's scale.

When you sweat, is it to prove
you don't reek of daisies?

When you see your sideline
sirens, prancing with pompoms
like double-fisted dandelions,
do you know you're planted
in the same field?

YOU MAKE ME FEEL LIKE DOING A SWAN DIVE

into an above-ground pool
full of Heaven Hill vodka.
Because your Absolut hateful
has ruined the expensive taste in my mouth.

The way you absolutely think you can decide,
        have decided,
everything about me and my gender,

which is a Styrofoam cup of Coke in the secret mini-fridge in my head.
You keep trying to tell me it's Diet Lemon,
when it's obviously Waffle House Cherry.

[Diet Lemon was discontinued in 2005]

I'm the only one who's tasted my secret,
mini-fridge Cherry Coke, goddammit.
To me, you're like that weed-flavored incense
I saw on Amazon-dot-com that one time.

You keep fucking burning, covering up
weed smell with artificial weed smell,
which I bet causes cancer instead of treating it-
        or fibromyalgia, whatever the shit that is.
You should make my life easier.

You should be, to me, like those conveniently-placed mud puddles
where Brad Pitt tossed his cigarettes in *Fight Club*,
which isn't at all unrealistic
because everyone knows
there were more puddles in the nineties.

But this isn't the nineties, and you're an asshole-
not even a bleached one.
When I'm around you, my happiness is the cheap-ass polish on my nails.

It's shiny red perfect for a toilet flush of time,
then you call me *he* seven or thirteen times,
chipping it away and now I look like a crack whore.
Even crack whores bleach their assholes.

NIGHTMARE ON GENDER STREET

I'm just sitting there in my living room, dreamily petting my golden retriever, who's wearing a goldfish costume—not cracker kind, but floats upside down kind—and I look down at my couch, which is made of salmon sushi. My Chuck Taylors are stuck to the sticky rice that spilled on the floor. That's when I hear children, who are dressed like it's the Fifties, even though this dream was filmed in Nineteen Eighty-Seven.

They sing, "One, two, the binary's coming for you. Three, four, get called "he" some more. Five, six, gotta go home to piss. Seven, eight, live in a body you hate. Nine, ten, this is copyright infringement."

Then a hole smokes through the floor, and my now-supportive mother leaps out of it. She's wearing a brown fedora and a red-green striped Christmas sweater. The nails on her right hand are as long as steak knives. Thank God, she's straight.

She says, "You look clownish when you wear makeup, bitch."

She swipes at me with her hetero nails, and I rip my feet free from the sticky rice somehow, but my geometric-patterned sweater still stinks like fish. It clashes with the Aquanet smell of my hair. I run down the hall, and all the pictures on the walls are of me in puffy-sleeved prom dresses and, in every one, you can see the bulge between my thighs. I barely notice the cheesy synthesizers in the background.

I hear Freddy, I mean, my mom shout, "You act stereotypically male, but you wear transvestite clothing, bitch."

Tears rip across my cheeks. I look down at the floor, which is tiled with plates of pecan cobbler. My mom laughs as she passes the thermostat and cranks up the heat, making the melting dessert stick to the soles of my shoes even worse. I can't exactly run anymore,and my mom starts to catch up with me as she sprints sideways along the wall, shattering the frames of my fake prom pictures.

She says, "Real women have periods, bitch."

I reach a dead end: the door to a public restroom. I turn around, and my mom stands so close, that I smell the beef brisket she's been cooking.

She says, "I will always love you, and you will always be my son. It's not my fault that you were born male, bitch."

She claws a hole through my geometric-patterned sweater, cutting a bloody number one through my skin. She gets a baby boy blue magic marker out of her purse, and writes an *XY* on my cheek as I feel hair poke through every pore. She reaches out her straight girl claws, about to trace the *XY* and scar me for life, when a giant version of my mascara bursts through the wall. It has a shiny pink cape, and the arms of a female body builder. It pulls a TV through the hole in the wall and holds it up with one arm as it turns on *Law and Order*, distracting my mom, who puts her face so close to the screen, her breath ghosts into condensation on the glass.

She says, "That's my favorite show, bitch."

Then, my mascara bashes her over the head with the TV, and she goes down quicker than my self-esteem during Thanksgiving dinner.

I say, "Mascara, thanks. But you didn't have to bludgeon my mom. Wait, why is there a smoke machine in here? Is it set to 'turbo?'"

Mom jumps back up like a drunk who just won't stay passed out. Her claws look longer than flag poles. My mascara is gone back through the hole it left in the floral wallpaper, and I have to bite my lip to keep my teeth from chattering until I hear her question.

She says, "By the way, bitch- how does someone like you even have sex?"

I say, "I am a glitterbomb of cunnilingus."

She screams as she melts into a puddle of fleshy goo, and it's uglier than the hairstyles at a pro-life rally. All that's left is that damn fedora.

LONELY, LONELY

I want to watch *The Girl with the Dragon Tattoo*
with my head in her lap.

I want to kiss along her perfect jawline,
and then argue
about who has better cheekbones.

I want to sit across the table from her,
and talk until the restaurant closes
and they take our cabernet from us,
even though there's a sip or two left.

When I undress her for the first time,
I want to look down at her body,
and tell her she's beautiful-
even if it turns out
that she has three breasts and labia down to her knees.

I hope she won't mind that I can't take my underwear off during sex.

I want her to leave a trail of potato chips
towards my bed
like they're rose petals.
I know that's how you get ants
But I'd call them my love raisins.

We'll listen to "Baby, Baby" by Amy Grant
with her thighs on my shoulders,

while she rides my face like
a surfboard in a hurricane—

kind of like how Amy treated
the probably-goateed mouth
of the man who inspired that song.

I know it's a different tongue motion,
but I feel like Amy Grant is a bad kisser.

Here I am, sitting in my apartment, alone,
even though I can take someone's bra off with one hand.

I think people who flirt with me are being nice,
and people who are being nice are flirting.
I either accidentally twat-block,

or I hit on friendly uninterested women
       and feel like dog shit covered in bird shit about it,
       but also like there aren't dumpsters
       deep enough to catch all my tears,
            but also more confused than someone
            who can't figure out why Amy Grant
            also uses her nose and chin while making out.

I stare at my reflection in my apartment window
as hail clinks against all the cars on my street,
wondering what's wrong with me,
and whether or not I'm cute enough.

"Baby, Baby" plays on my stereo,
and I make tiny practice circles with my tongue.
I do it inside my mouth, so my neighbors don't think I'm weird.

OVER BEFORE IT BEGINS AGAIN

Before I throw the head-hung, wilted roses into the campfire,
I grip the thorns in my fist, just so I can appreciate the sting.
I fling them into the flames and think to myself,
"Shit, I must be real sad."
I'm alone out here, and no bear even gives enough of a shit
to stop by and maul me.

The jar of peach-flavored Arkansas lightning is empty.
I just went fishing, and I dipped my feet in the water the whole time,
and the coolness and the mud between my toes
wasn't enough to invert my frown. I didn't catch anything,
not even a Budweiser can, or a crack pipe
even though I'm still technically in Little Rock.

I see a glob of sunscreen on my arm,
even though I haven't put any on since I left my one-bedroom.
I sniff it, and it turns out to be bird shit.
Even if I'd caught that shit yesterday when it was still worms,
it would have wriggled through my hands
before I could bait my hook with it-

which is how I feel about her. Her eyes, brown like milk chocolate,
are my wonder wall still, but now I'm baker's chocolate bitter.
The sable of the midnight pine trees is mulch compared to her hair.
I still think it's dreamy as fuck that she doesn't shave her arms,

even though the moss-thick fuzz reaches her knuckles,
and she says she doesn't care if it makes people think she's trans.
Trans like me. But she's with him, and he has what I have to live without.

Mascara is smeared across my face like the war paint
from a battle that left all my troops with missing legs.
Yes, I even wear mascara when I'm alone in the woods. Fight me.

Anyway, I hope she's happier than a bear waking from hibernation
to a hummingbird spring, or a bear dancing in a leather bar,
or a bear that got off his woodland, grizzly ass long enough
to tear me up like a damn tissue. I can't waste any more time on her.

I need to be out here, alone,
watching the roses burn, and drunkenly strumming
on my banjo, my thorn-bitten fingertips
stumbling blood across the fretboard
as my thumb ring snaps the thumb string. Fuck these flowers,

I should have saved the six bucks. Thank god
I didn't spend more on some boy-fucker.
What will the people at Walmart think
when I go in there alone next time? I'll walk past their cheap roses,
straight to the game and fish section. I'll buy a can of worms instead.

CONCRETE EDEN

Because it's me, I've been crying.
I look in the mirror and, after wiping tears away,
then resting my forehead on my palm,

I've smeared eyeliner into the shape of a cross like Ash Wednesday.
It looks like ashes. No candles are lit,
and I haven't been to church since
the first teal tab of estrogen sat like a communion wafer,
chalky against my tongue.

I remember when you and I were nineteen,
and we got roped into being acolytes at my small, childless church,
tying cords around our robed waists.

Now you crossed paths with a westbound Texas train,
splitting and smearing, making yourself into the arms of a bloody cross.

We are Adam and Lilith,
but you're the one that left the concrete Eden of Little Rock,
with its Baptist churches on every corner,
next to every bullet-peppered patio,
next to every Evan Williams-filled liquor store.

You are the one who left me for Samael,
the angel of death, who spread his bony wings
and dragged you through cornfields to Texarkana.

Because your new beginning only led to your end.
Because now I'm beginning to think of biting
into this apple of original sin,
filled with the of cowboy killers and forty-ounce Budweisers
and cocaine.

Because I am alone and I am thirsty to join you.
Because the serpent told me so.

Because I want to drag myself down just a little further,
so I can at least understand.
You ended your life, and left barbecue joints, brewpubs,
your mother, a sister, and me.

You were the only man I will ever love, but couldn't.
I can't help but top Eve, instead of laying with you.
Still, you were the one who was supposed to grow old with me,

dying our grey hair green and teaching our grandkids
about nihilism and Nietzsche.
Now you're stuck at twenty-eight, dead.
Your laugh is what I miss the most.
I snicker as I bite into the apple, taste the ash and cheap beer.
I snort lines off your picture,
each one covering your eyes.

IT STARTS LIKE A COUNTRY SONG

You failed trucker school
because you got petrified like a stag in headlights,
and ran eighteen wheels over a Styrofoam doe.
With a bank account scraped clean like an empty peanut butter jar,
you had to move to a hick town in Texas,

the kind where convenience stores sell cock-stiff cowboy hats
next to confederate flag belt buckles
that'll break apart the second
they're used to crack open Shiner beer bottles.

You had to move to a hick town in Texas
to be a live-in nanny for your sister's kids.
I can just picture you,

lecturing three year-olds on the joys
of existential nihilism
as you spread strawberry jelly across a slice of Wonderbread,
which you compare to the Bangkok sweatshop
bloodshed that is capitalism.

Capitalism having gotten in the way,
after your husband divorced you-
the husband who supported you like a leaking water bra
when you quit your job as manager of the Fried Chicken Barn

to stay home and write poetry that would get Nietzsche's nipples hard.

Your ex-husband is keeping his Walmart paychecks all to himself now.
The two of you were my first gay wedding reception,
but not my first gay wedding.

But it was my first experience with Mong culture,
because your husband's immigrant family's double-wide
was a Laotian dive bar.
I was unfamiliar with the Mong tradition of drinking
until all the liquor's gone, taking turns taking shots one-by-one.
Otherwise, I would have brought a smaller bottle of Wild Turkey.

We felt so grown up, having known each other
before we knew we were both queer.

It was sweeter than a bowl of Lucky Charms
when your head followed the rainbow onto my shoulder
the night after high school graduation,
when we were smoking that corn,
or maybe it was Reggie.

It was sweet, even though I rejected your advances.
            Even though, darling, there is nothing I'd rather do
                than love you,

I shrugged you off me like throwing away
an unscratched, winning lottery ticket.

Because sometimes boys grow up to be girls,
and sometimes girls like girls,
no matter how amazing the boys in their lives are.

You spent ten years two Johnny Cash songs
away from my house in Little Rock,
and now you're on the other side of Texarkana,
wrist deep in off-brand crayons. While I'm stuck here,

in my transphobic parents' upstairs,
wearing a 3XL Garth Brooks T-shirt

71

to hide the fact that I'm getting boobs at age 26-
until I can move into the apartment complex down the street.
Here we sit, shooting text messages back and forth
like an off-brand rainbow between our flip phones,
arching across a million rows of corn,
a thousand Walmarts,
ten dudes named Cooter,
and more roadkill possums than there are spots
on our matching, leopard print Snuggies.

Maybe someday soon,
we'll meet under the peak of the technicolor semicircle
in a rural gay bar called The Bedazzled Gun Rack.
Trisha Queerwood might could pull up in her baby pink F-150
and put on a drag show.

PRIDE

When the doctor asked me if I had a gun in my apartment,
I knew she was about to give me the good shit.

She handed me a clipboard questionnaire
to help people figure out if they're sad enough to be medicated.
If your answer on a scale from zero to three is mostly zeros,
then you've probably never collapsed in the fetal position,
sobbing like a thousand dogs died in a thousand movies
        at your fucking job.
I answered mostly threes.

She asked me how I would off myself,
and I said I'd cut my wrists up in the bathtub,
but I don't have a drain-stopper.

Doing that without filling the tub with water first
would be too sticky and gross.

I try to fill the awkward silence
by saying that I want to start a new slang term.
Instead of "commit suicide,"
I want people to start saying, "hang a suey."

That filled the silence like Cherry Skoal Uncut
fills the lip of a man who just lost his jaw to cancer.

She asked me what the main source of my depression was,
and if there's something I hold onto in order to stay alive.
I tell her that they are the same thing.

I tell her, "My best friend shotgunned his brains
across the inside of a toolshed.
I know what that did to me,
and I cannot do that to anyone else."

73

She scribbles that in her notes.

He was the first person I knew who wrote poetry,
and the first person I knew
who was out
as anything.

When I told my grandmother he committed suicide,
she asked me if he was Transgender,
I told her, "No, he wasn't."

However, he was and is the father to my queerness.
He showed me that life exists outside of the closet,
but you do have to reach in there
to grab a sweater every once in a while.

When my grandmother asked me that,
it only reminded me that I cannot be
another trans person to commit suicide.

The world needs people like me to rid itself of the gender binary
like it was those blonde highlights
that look like they came from a box
you found under your sink
after half a jar of peach moonshine.

My friend wasn't transgender,
but I feel like all queers do that to the binary.
Even when I start to believe the voice in the back of my skull
that says I'm worthless,
that I'm cheaper than a stolen bottle of Heaven Hill,

at least I have the gender binary moonshine blonde thing.

That, at least, is a start.
That, at least, is the first step to staying alive.
Especially when so many others have died too young.

Especially when slurs
like faggot, tranny, and dyke
were the last ones some of us heard.

That, to me, is what pride is.
So I got help.

ODE TO A MULLET

Her gray hair was spiked
and sprayed in the front,
with a long mousse-filled
mane in the back.

I respected her
for it. It made no
attempt to taper
to the long part,

which hit me like a
runaway trailer.
I respected her
for it. You know

people were telling
her to get a new
haircut way before
Bill Clinton did

not have sexual
relations with that
woman. But every
morning, she works

that Aquanet; looks
in that mirror; and
says, "Sweet Jesus. I
make this look good."

GAY BACON LETTUCE AND TOMATO

I tell my female friend that I'm jealous
of how gay men's culture seems like one giant martini glass,
whereas being a trans and/or queer woman
involves a lot of marching in the street and generally being angry.
She tells me that's just part of being a woman
and men are ruled by their libidos.

My guy friend tells me that my transition inspires him,
and I tell him that he inspires me every time
he does a guy in the butt.

I don't understand how accessing the medical care I need
is the same as God's footsteps on the fucking beach.

It's not inspirational when I put on tucking underwear
so that there is no bulge in my men's briefs
before I look in the mirror and tell myself that I am a real lesbian,
not a straight man who's also a really casual drag queen.

I think of all the straight men I feel that I must compete with
for the hearts of pansexual women
        or bisexual
        or queer
        or switch hitter
        or whatever they call themselves these days.

Except these dudes always win,
even if they have three roommates and no car.
Then I'm left worrying that I'm biphobic for thinking this
about whoever I was just trying to date.

I tried making out with guys,
but I felt dust collecting in my phantom vagina both times.
Turns out I only thought I was into them
because I want long fingernails
instead of sex chicklets.

I think about how my chances of getting beaten
like I was a man
or getting murdered would increase
if I dated them.

Especially if I was a trans woman of color
instead of just saying their names
when they get stabbed by some fucking chaser.

But I'm depressed because I've only gone down on two women this year-
that I've only been on dates with five,
when I wish I got laid like Shane from *The L Word*.

But then I feel like a bad feminist for wanting that.

Does texting them the next morning
to say that they're awesome but I'm emotionally unavailable
really make me any better than men
who treat women like fuckable cheeseburgers?

At least I try to be friends with them after,
which isn't something you do with a cheeseburger.
And I'm only unavailable because I'm always hung up on someone
like sneakers on power lines.

Do you ever punch yourself in the boob just to know you're alive?

IF YOU NEED ME

You're always opening doors for me,
and I love how it makes me feel so dainty.
Today, your arms
were full,

and you covered your blushing cheeks
by joking that, since I followed you
all the way down the hall to the door,
you might as well let me open it for you.

I used it as an opportunity
to look down and compliment your cherry-patterned dress.

For me, getting out in all that humidity
feels like walking into a giant sheet of saran wrap.
You always remind me to slow down and breathe
when I'm anxious.

You won't let me say I'm fine when I'm not.
When you're sad, it's worth burning down

the entire state of Arkansas
with a used-up,
sputtering lighter
to see you smile again.

But when you're sad,
you stand

with the sun at your radiant back
like nothing's wrong.
But if your knees should give out,
I'll catch you.

If you need me,
I'll catch you.

If you need me,
I'll catch you.
If you need me,
I'll catch you.

I won't see you until you walk
back through those doors.

Until then, you'll pulsate through my mind
like the rhythmic wails of locusts.
I've already tried to be more
than what I am to you,

and you didn't want that, and that's okay.
But if you ever need me.

DON'T IT FEEL LIKE DECEMBER

This Christmas, Rudolph is venison
heated up in the microwave.
My sister isn't flying home from New York City,

and the closest I'm getting to making a trip up north
is the Milwaukee's Best in my left hand.
I wonder if our family thinks she jumped on the gay wagon
because of me.

If I could turn people gay,
Arkansas would be a rainbow of carabiner clips.

All the fights I've had with my folks-
each of those memories is a petal on a rose
that smells like Santa Claus shit.

If I could save my sister from having that one big fight with Mom,
and the months of awkwardly latching
onto friends' moms like bananas in pudding.
I wish Mom realized it's fine that she's queer.

Hell, she should've seen it coming.

Growing up, me and my sister used to wear each other's clothes.
Me in a mauve tank top and yellow daisy dukes,
her in baggy jeans and a trucker hat, just felt right-
unless it was too hot outside for my wig.

Right now it's too cold for cockroaches,
and that only reminds me that I need to buy a new calendar.
I wish I could protect my sister from all of this with a sapphic shield.
I would've thought going through that with me
would've made it easier for her—

that they might paint a pink triangle on the back of their SUV
and parade through town with us in the backseat.
I see the multi-colored Christmas lights tangled around
the gun rack on my neighbor's broke down truck,
and I ask myself, *Don't it feel like December now?*
And I pretend he doesn't keep them on all year round.

Things will work out eventually. As for what won't,
that's why God made Zoloft.

ABOUT THE POET

Lilith Mae McFarlin lives in North Little Rock, Arkansas with her parrot, Polly. She works in a public library and enjoys playing the banjo while complaining about the patriarchy.

ABOUT THE PRESS

Sibling Rivalry Press is an independent press based in Little Rock, Arkansas. It is a sponsored project of Fractured Atlas, a nonprofit arts service organization. Contributions to support the operations of Sibling Rivalry Press are tax-deductible to the extent permitted by law, and your donations will directly assist in the publication of work that disturbs and enraptures. To contribute to the publication of more books like this one, please visit our website and click *donate*.

Sibling Rivalry Press gratefully acknowledges the following donors, without whom this book would not be possible:

Anonymous (18)
Arkansas Arts Council
John Bateman
W. Stephen Breedlove
Dustin Brookshire
Sarah Browning
Billy Butler
Asher Carter
Don Cellini
Nicole Connolly
Jim Cory
Risa Denenberg
John Gaudin
In Memory of Karen Hayes
Gustavo Hernandez
Amy Holman
Jessica Jacobs & Nickole Brown
Paige James
Nahal Suzanne Jamir
Allison Joseph
Collin Kelley
Trevor Ketner

Andrea Lawlor
Anthony Lioi
Ed Madden & Bert Easter
Mitchell, Blackstock, Ivers & Sneddon, PLLC
Stephen Mitchell
National Endowment for the Arts
Stacy Pendergrast
Simon Randall
Paul Romero
Randi M. Romo
Carol Rosenfeld
Joseph Ross
In Memory of Bill Rous
Matthew Siegel
Alana Smoot
Katherine Sullivan
Tony Taylor
Leslie Taylor
Hugh Tipping
Guy Traiber
Mark Ward
Robert Wright